FINDING TREASURE

A Collection of Collections

Michelle Schaub

Illustrated by Carmen Saldaña

Charlesbridge

To Matt, my treasure—M. S.
Para David y Maria: vosotros sabéis por qué—C. S.

Text copyright © 2019 by Michelle Schaub
Illustrations copyright © 2019 by Carmen Saldaña
All rights reserved, including the right of reproduction in whole or in part in any form.
Charlesbridge and colophon are registered trademarks of Charlesbridge Publishing, Inc.

At the time of publication, all URLs printed in this book were accurate and active. Charlesbridge, the author, and the illustrator are not responsible for the content or accessibility of any website.

Published by Charlesbridge
85 Main Street
Watertown, MA 02472
(617) 926-0329
www.charlesbridge.com

Library of Congress Cataloging-in-Publication Data
Names: Schaub, Michelle, author. | Saldaña, Carmen, illustrator.
Title: Finding Treasure: a collection of collections / Michelle Schaub; illustrated by
    Carmen Saldaña.
Description: Watertown, MA: Charlesbridge, [2019] | Summary: Told in rhyming text,
    a child approaches a school assignment by exploring the collections of family members
    and friends, and embarking on a personal quest to develop a collection. Includes a note
    and suggestions for children starting a collection.
Identifiers: LCCN 2017059679 (print) | LCCN 2018001386 (ebook) |
    ISBN 9781632896995 (ebook) | ISBN 9781632897008 (ebook pdf) |
    ISBN 9781580898751 (reinforced for library use)
Subjects: LCSH: Collectors and collecting—Juvenile fiction. | Hobbies—Juvenile fiction. |
    Stories in rhyme. | CYAC: Stories in rhyme. | Collectors and collecting—Fiction. |
    Hobbies—Fiction. | LCGFT: Stories in rhyme. | Picture books.
Classification: LCC PZ8.3.S297122 (ebook) | LCC PZ8.3.S297122 Co 2019 (print) |
    DDC [E]—dc23
LC record available at https://lccn.loc.gov/2017059679

Printed in China
(hc) 10 9 8 7 6 5 4 3 2 1

Illustrations done in digital media
Display type set in Hayseed by Typadelic Fonts
Text type set in Colby Narrow by Jason Vandenberg
Color separations by Colourscan Print Co. Pte. Ltd, Singapore
Printed by 1010 Printing International Limited in Huizhou, Guangdong, China
Production supervision by Brian G. Walker
Designed by Diane M. Earley

My Collection Conundrum

My teacher gave us homework
that has me quite perplexed.
He asked us all to bring to class
something we collect.
It seems that everyone BUT ME
knows just the thing to share.
"My jar of marbles."
"Arrowheads."
"My favorite teddy bears."

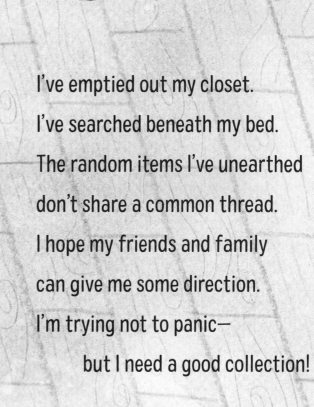

I've emptied out my closet.

I've searched beneath my bed.

The random items I've unearthed

don't share a common thread.

I hope my friends and family

can give me some direction.

I'm trying not to panic—

but I need a good collection!

My Mother's Button Box

Shiny ones
    of shell and glass.
Pearly circles,
    swirls of brass.
Anchors snipped
    from navy coats.
Plastic hearts,
    wooden boats.
Daisies, paisleys,
    bugs, and bows.
Bunnies saved
    from baby clothes.
A potpourri
    of shapes and hues.
My favorite one?
Too hard to choose!

My Father's Trains

Round and round the crisscrossed lanes,
engines pull my father's trains.
Boxcars, tankers in a row,
circus cars with beasts in tow,
flatcars hauling toys and cranes.

Trailing, one caboose remains,
the last link in this vintage chain,
rumbling past the old depot,

Loop on loop, momentum gains.
Cars whir past like hurricanes.
Signals flash and whistles blow.
I love to watch the dizzy show
when Daddy runs his model trains,

Sissy's Snow Globes

Lacy flakes
whirl and twirl
round towns
and lakes.

Where is that bridge?
That mountain ridge?
That stately statue, too?

They're blurred in a
swirling
snowflake stew.

What a view!

When confetti settles like sprinkles on a cake,
time to make it snow again—
Just tip, and . . .

Shake!
Shake!
Shake!

My Brothers and Their Baseball Cards

"I've got an all-star lineup."

"My players are top rate."

"This batter's stats are stellar."

"This catcher's record's great."

"I like your brand-new rookie;
his future's looking bright."

*"Here's a fielder in his prime.
Wanna trade?"*

"I might."

"How 'bout for your vintage card,
the one from Grandpa Pete?"

"The legendary pitcher?"

"He really threw some heat."

"I'll swap, but for your shortstop, too—
the one that you got signed."

"Toss in that second baseman,
and then I wouldn't mind."

"He's a Hall of Famer.
Now, really, that's a steal . . ."

"But I'll throw in that rookie card.
Shake hands?"

"It's a deal!"

Grandpa's Good Cents

Whenever he spies
a glint of silver
hiding in a sidewalk crack
or
a flash of copper
dropped in the street,
he stops.
He picks it up
and squints
to check the year
and note the mint,
hoping to find
a buffalo nickel,
a Roosevelt dime,
or some other bright prize
to make his set complete.
Gramps always says,
"Keep your eyes open wide—
for the treasure you seek
could be right
　　at
　　　your
　　　　feet."

Granny's Teapots

So prim and proper,

they perch atop cabinets,

adorned in party dresses.

Roses,

pinstripes,

polka dots.

Some tall and thin,

some short and squat.

All pose,

one arm akimbo,

the other pointing high—

waiting,

patient,

while I choose:

Which will host

our tea for two?

Whose Forgotten Treasures?

Stashed in the attic,

a small shadow box

holds rows of old keys

long lost from their locks.

Fashioned of iron

with patterns ornate.

What might they open?

Which cupboard? Which gate?

The latch to a castle
or secret château?
A wardrobe that leads
to a land white with snow?

These keys are enchanting;
yes, I'll admit.
But a treasure for me?
They're not the right fit.

Auntie Kate's Vanity PL8TS

BUCKLUP

DNTBSLW

LUV2ZIP

TIME2GO

CELEBR8

Y B BLU

L8 TER

G8 TER

B C N U

Aunt Nisha's Nature Display

Polished pebbles gleam,
dreaming of the smooth caress
of whispering streams.

A prickly brown pile
of pinecone armadillos
wear sticky sap scales.

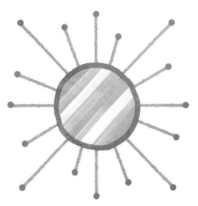

Such delicate shells!
Spiral halls hide a surprise:
the deep, roaring sea.

Asher's Aquariums

My cousin keeps amazing fish
and creatures of the sea.
I like to help him feed them
while he tallies them for me.
"It started with **1** guppy
I won at the school fair.
I added **2** pink ramshorn snails;
my fish tank still felt bare.
3 platys joined the party,
peppered orange and black,
and then **4** tiny catfish
that like to hide in back.

(They love the **5** aquatic ferns
that sway so peacefully.)
There goes my molly school of **6**;
they're marbled, did you see?
I had to buy another tank
for **7** sunken ships,
8 tetras, and **9** danios—
watch them dart and dip!
10 cleaner shrimp complete my crew,
but only for today.
One thing I didn't count on—
new babies on the way!"

Meg's Menagerie

When I peek round my friend Meg's room,

this is what I see:

      pandas,

      penguins,

      zebras, too—

all looking back at me.

A bookshelf packed with orca whales.

A desktop with dalmatians.

And in a spot of honor—skunks,

her current fascination.

What fuels my friend's affinity?

What brings her such delight?

The reason is unclear to me,

but to Meg

it's **black** and white.

Roger's Roosts

Cheer-a-lees, fee-dee-dees,
robins and chickadees
love Roger's birdhouses;
so do the wrens.

Merrily from each tree,
legions of homes swing free,
perfectly sized for his
fine feathered friends.

My Mail Carrier's Cache

The items postman Ray collects
are not at all what I'd expect.
No stamps of fancy birds or ships.
No postcards from exotic trips.
When he pulls mail from his old tote,
he watches faces and takes note.
Ray makes his rounds on time despite
the snow and rain and gloom of night
because, across the well-worn miles,
he's energized by saved-up **smiles.**

Mae's Stock of Clocks

The Rise and Shine Diner—

no bistro is finer.

The menu has quite a selection.

The food is inviting,

but just as exciting,

the owner's alarm-clock collection.

Mae's crammed several cases

with ticktocking faces

that ring with a synchronized chime.

The clocks and the crowd

are a little bit loud,

but our orders are always on time.

The Gist of Collecting

Who gathers flies without disgust?

A **dip**-ter-**ol**-o-**gist**.

Who saves and studies lunar dust?

A **sel**-en-**ol**-o-gist.

Who hunts for footprints fossilized?

Ich-**nol**-o-**gists**, it's true.

Who seeks out fungi, any size?

My-**col**-o-**gists** sure do.

Some collectors specialize;

their goals are quite specific.

Ask.

    Observe.

        Hypothesize.

Their method?

    Scientific.

Collecting Stars?

When darkness deepens,

sparks of starlight

dance around the yard.

They beckon,

Come and catch us!

I fill a mason jar

and watch the embers

flash and glow,

    but . . .

     I know . . .

      though it's hard . . .

these specks of light

aren't mine to keep.

     So   float   free—

good-bye, stars!

My Treasure Found

I've started a collection!

I know what brings me joy!

Forget about rare heirlooms

or captivating toys.

My treasures aren't from nature.

No pebbles, shells, or twigs.

I haven't salvaged gizmos

or quirky whirligigs.

My medley isn't common,

nor is it very strange.

It isn't something that you count,

sort, or rearrange.

But it can kindle stories

or spark a memory.

Gathered up inside this

book:

my favorite . . .

POETRY!

Let the Collecting Begin!

All over the world, people collect items as common as key chains and as rare as four-leaf clovers. Why are so many hooked on this hobby? Is it the thrill of the hunt? The chance to preserve the past? Maybe it's because collections are memory keepers. Every time a new item is added to a collection, a story is captured. Later, when looking over a collection or sharing it with a friend, you can tell those stories. Why did an item catch your eye? Where and when did you find it? Who once owned it? What was its purpose? A collection is a unique record of interests, adventures, wishes, and whims.

Ready to get started? Here are a few tips:

Tap Into Your Passion: Think about what makes you happy and fuels your fascination. Learning about the solar system? Folding origami animals? Searching for shells on a beach? Collecting should be fun, so choose something you love.

Keep Your Eyes Open Wide: Building your collection is a treasure hunt. Be observant when you're out and about, especially in new places. You never know when you'll find a new prize!

Be Patient: A great collection doesn't appear overnight. It may take years to build, especially if you gather rare items like historic coins or vintage toys.

Make It Unique: As your collection grows, find ways to make it special. Have you collected Santa Claus figures? Try zooming in on blue Santas. Do you enjoy comic books? Narrow in on those featuring a particular character. Focusing will add a challenge. It will also limit the number of items, so your collection doesn't grow out of control.

Sort It Out: Decide how to organize your collection. Will you arrange your giraffe statues by size? Your baseball caps by league? If you collect small items like buttons or sea glass, you might even create a mosaic to hang as art. Let your creativity guide you.

Share Your Flair: Display your collection so others can enjoy it. Set up a shelf in your room? Create an album? Reserve exhibit space at your local library? One way to share your passion is to join a club. There are collectors' clubs for almost any category, from action figures to zeppelin models. You can find a list of organizations at **www.collectoronline.com**. Don't see a club for you on the list? Start your own!